NEW MILLENNIUM KIDS PUBLISHING

Creative and Crafty Writing

The fun and easy way to get kids to write for God's glory!

a 12-lesson, Christian course combining writing lessons and cool crafts

By Karine Bauch and Jan May

Student Workbook

© Karine Bauch and Jan May 2017. All rights reserved.

Creative and Crafty Writing (Student Workbook) by Karine Bauch and Jan May
Copyright © Karine Bauch and Jan May, 2008, 2017.

All rights reserved. No part of this book may be used or reproduced in any manner whatsoever without written permission, except where noted within the text.

Printed in the United States of America

First edition

Scripture quotations are taken from the Holy Bible, *New Living Translation*, copyright 1996, 2004. Used by permission of Tyndale House Publishers, Inc., Wheaton, Illinois 60189. All rights reserved.

Published by New Millennium Girl Books
690 Laurel Drive
Aurora, IL 60506

ISBN 978-0-9801708-8-7

Cover Design: Karine Bauch

Illustrations provided by www.clipart.com

Raymond Kelly at www.Spitewell.com
Ocean - http://www.whimsyclips.com/
Laura Martinez
http://www.teacherspayteachers.com/Store/Teacher-Laura
© Graphics Created by the 3AM Teacher   http://the3amteacher.blogspot.com/
http://www.teacherspayteachers.com/Store/Janelle-Web

Table of Contents

Lesson 1. 5

Lesson 2. 9

Lesson 3. 13

Lesson 4 15

Lesson 5 19

Lesson 6. 22

Lesson 7 24

Lesson 8 31

Lesson 9 33

Lesson 10 34

Lesson 11 36

Lesson 12 39

Hello Student!

You are about to start a creative journey as your learn to write for God's glory! You will create a "Treasure Journal" during the first class and use it for doing optional homework assignments. They are listed below in order:

Lesson One: Write about a time in your life that was an adventure. It can be as simple as a romp in the woods or as elaborate as a trip overseas. Be as descriptive as possible!

Lesson Two: Write a list of 12 descriptive words or phrases for each of the following places: the beach, your bedroom and outer space.

Lesson Three: Write a list of 5 words or phrases that describe how you feel when you are in each of the following places: your backyard, the dentist's office, and the arms of a loving relative.

Lesson Four: Write about an event in your life that was a shock or a surprise to you. It could be something happy, like a surprise party, or a sad event, like the loss of a grandparent.

Lesson Five: Write two lists of descriptive words that tell about both the current season and the upcoming one.

Lesson Six: Think of a favorite adult in your life and write out three lists of words or phrases that describe his or her: LIKES, DISLIKES, and ACTIVITIES.

Lesson Seven: Interview an adult about one of the following events in his or her life: his first day of school, the day she met her spouse, or his most embarrassing moment. Write it out as a story.

Lesson Eight: Write a made up story about yourself in your journal that starts like this: "If everything goes right today, then..." Don't be afraid to describe your biggest dreams for the day!

Lesson Nine: Write out a made up conversation between you and a famous person from either the present or past. Try NOT to make it an interview, but rather a discussion of a topic that is well known to the person.

Lesson Ten: Write a true or fictional story about yourself that starts with the following sentence: "The sun rose this morning, just like every other morning, but I had no idea that this day would change my life..."

Lesson Eleven: Create titles for the last three days of your life. Examples: "The Day We Filled the Fridge", or "Math Madness".

Lesson One

"Outside show is a poor substitute for inner worth."
-Aesop

WRITING A FABLE WORKSHEET
Fill in the following worksheet to begin your fable.

1. Choose a Moral:
    a. "If At First You Don't Succeed, Try, Try Again"
    b. "Haste Makes Waste"
    c. "If You Don't Work, You Don't Eat"
    d. Make Up Your Own :
    _____

2. Choose an animal that will learn this:
   _____

3. Why did he need to learn this? Was he lazy, grumpy, impatient, greedy, or selfish?
   _____

4. What does your animal look like?
    a. Size: _____
    b. Color: _____
    c. Texture (Furry, soft, smooth): _____
    d. Can you use any similes?
        i. "He was as tall as a tree."
        ii. "She was as round as a ball."
        iii. _____
             _____

5. Who are the other animals that will help him learn the lesson? Choose only a few. Describe them briefly:
   _____
   _____
   _____
   _____

6. Choose a setting: forest, mountains, cave, tree, town, etc.
   _____

a. What is it like there? Make a list of all the things that you would experience there: Remember to include colors!

See	Hear	Taste	Smell	Touch

7. How will the animal learn this lesson? Create an obstacle:

_____
_____
_____
_____
_____
_____
_____

TREASURE JOURNAL CLIPART
Cut out or copy these treasure map pictures for your treasure journal. Add some of your own, too!

Lesson Two

> *"Anyone with ears to hear should listen and understand."*
> -Matt 13:23

Use the space below to write out your fable.

Title: _____

_____
_____
_____
_____
_____
_____
_____
_____
_____
_____
_____
_____
_____
_____
_____
_____

FABLE CLIPART PAGE

Either cut out or copy these pictures for your fable pop-up book.

Lesson Three

> *"To God belong wisdom and power; counsel and understanding are His."*
> Job 12:13

Write the final copy of your fable here and cut it out:

Lesson Four

NEWS STORY WORKSHEET (page 1)

> *So stop telling lies. Let us tell our neighbors the truth, for we are all parts of the same body.*
> Eph 4:25

1. Choose a well-known fairy tale or Bible story, such as:
   a. Red Riding Hood
   b. Cinderella
   c. Pinocchio
   d. The Three Pigs
   e. Sleeping Beauty
   f. Beauty and the Beast
   g. Peter Rabbit
   h. David and Goliath
   i. Noah's Ark
   j. Moses Parts the Red Sea
   k. Other: _____

2. Write out the FINAL result of the story:
   _____
   _____

3. From that result, fill in the following answers:
   a. Who: _____
   b. What: _____
   c. When: _____
   d. Where: _____
   e. Why: _____
   f. How: _____

4. What events led up to the final result (in order):
   a. _____
   b. _____
   c. _____
   d. _____

5. List any other details that you can think of about the main character. These can be made up, as long as it goes along with the story:
   a. _____
   b. _____

6. List any other details that you can think of about the other characters:
   a. Name: _____ Detail: _____
   b. Name: _____ Detail: _____
   c. Name: _____ Detail: _____
   d. Name: _____ Detail: _____

Now, write a short, catchy headline for the story:

_____

Draw a sunken ship into the picture, then color!

Pray for All People
I Tim 2:1

You will hear of wars and rumors of wars...but the end is still to come.
Matt 24:6

...good news gives health to the bones.
Prov 15:30

And the **gospel** must first be preached to all nations.
Mark 13:10

The earth is the LORD's,
and everything in it,
the world, and all who live in it.
Psalm 24:1

18

Lesson Five

> "They do not fear bad news; they confidently trust the Lord to care for them."
> Psalm 112:7

NEWS STORY WORKSHEET (Part 2)

1. **Start with your LEAD sentence.** It should tell the **WHO, WHAT, WHEN** and **WHERE** of the final result of the story. (See NEWS STORY WORKSHEET, #3, a, b, c and d from the last lesson.)

   _____
   _____
   _____

2. Your next sentence should tell **WHY**. (See news story worksheet #3 e.)

   _____
   _____

3. Your next sentence or two should tell **HOW**. (See news story worksheet #3 f.)

   _____
   _____

4. Let's start the second paragraph. **Tell the main events of the story in order**. Leave out unimportant details. (See news story worksheet #4.)

   _____
   _____
   _____
   _____
   _____
   _____
   _____

5. Write one more paragraph that includes some **details** about the various characters. (See news story worksheet #5 and #6.)

   _____
   _____
   _____
   _____
   _____
   _____
   _____
   _____

6. Give your workbook to your **teacher** to edit.

7. **Rewrite** the final draft neatly in the next section. Add a headline and an illustration. Cut it out of this book and give it to your teacher who will put them together into a newspaper.

Color me!

News Story (final draft)

WRITE YOUR HEADLINE HERE:

DRAW A PICTURE OF YOUR NEWS STORY HERE:

START WRITING YOUR STORY HERE:

Write the final copy of your news story on the lines to the left, starting in the first column.

Remember to **print neatly**!

Then, **cut out** the headline, drawing and story. Your teacher will put it together with other stories and make a whole newspaper!

Lesson Six

THEME AND SETTING WORKSHEET

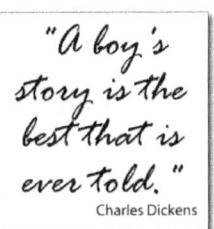

"A boy's story is the best that is ever told."
— Charles Dickens

Answer the following questions:

1. Which season have you chosen for your theme? _____
2. Can you think of a sub-theme to go with it?
   _____
3. Where is this story taking place?
   a. Country: _____
   b. State: _____
   c. City or town name: (can be fictitious)
      _____
   d. Neighborhood type (circle one):
      i. Suburbs
      ii. City
      iii. Rural

4. Make a list of the things that you might experience there. Remember to use vivid adjectives: color, size, emotion, etc.

Sights	Sounds	Smells	Tastes	Touch

Examples:

- puffy, white clouds
- happy, chattering birds
- damp, musty logs
- delicious, chicken salad

5. In which month and year will your story take place?

   Month: _____ Year: _____

Lesson Seven

CREATING A CHARACTER WORKSHEET

You don't have a soul. You are a Soul. You have a body.
— C.S. Lewis

1. Is your character a male or female? _____

2. How old is he or she? _____

3. What does he/she look like? Include some similes:

    "He was as tall as a tree"
    "Her eyes were as blue as sapphires"

    a. Hair: _____
    b. Eyes: _____
    c. Height: _____
    d. Other: _____

4. Does he/she have any special features? *big eyes, nose, or ears, missing teeth, ruby lips, squinty eyes, cheery smile, strength, hunched back, spiked hair*
    _____
    _____
    _____

5. How does he/she dress? *Sporty, messy, dressy, neat, unique*

    a. <u>Show, don't tell</u> how he/she is dressed: *"His shirt was hanging out and his pants were torn."* or *"She checked in the mirror to make sure she didn't have any wrinkles on her dress."*

    b. _____
       _____
       _____
       _____
       _____
       _____

6. What do you like about your character?
    _____
    _____
    _____

7. What don't you like about your character?
   _____
   _____
   _____

8. <u>Create a Personality:</u> Choose from the list or create some of your own. Circle the ones you like for your main character. **Show, don't tell** one sentence about five of the words you chose on the lines below:

Outgoing	Funny	Serious	Loud	Quiet
Smiles	Frowns	Glares	Strong	Weak
Brave	Shy	Afraid	Kind	Helpful
Playful	Silly	Sporty	Generous	Sassy
Spunky	Sneaky	Witty	Mean	Nice
Mysterious	Proud	Wise	Humble	Clumsy

Example:
   Spunky – She jumped up when her father came home.

   a. _____
   b. _____
   c. _____
   d. _____
   e. _____

What are some things he/she likes to do? *hunt, fish, play sports, watch birds, draw, sing, play an instrument:* _____

Craft Time

Let's create a face from the features on the following pages.

Create a Character!

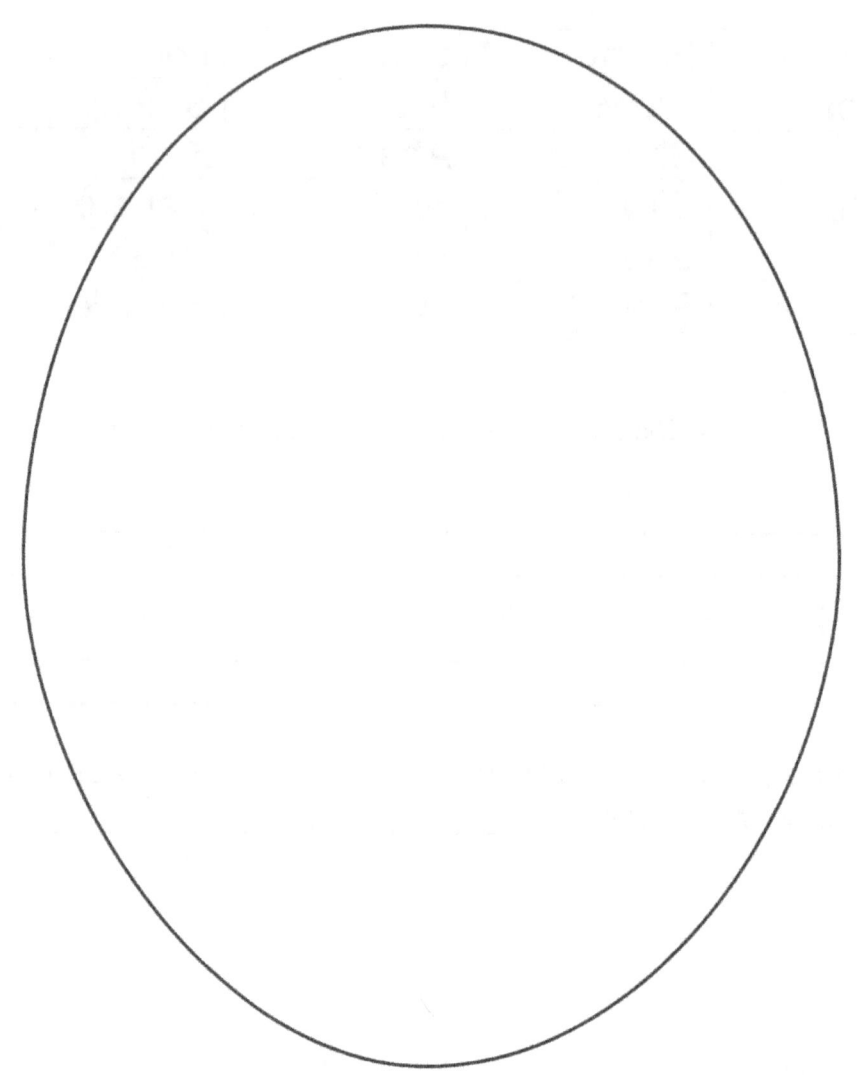

Add eyes, nose, mouth, ears and hair!
Cut out clipart or draw your own.

Eyes

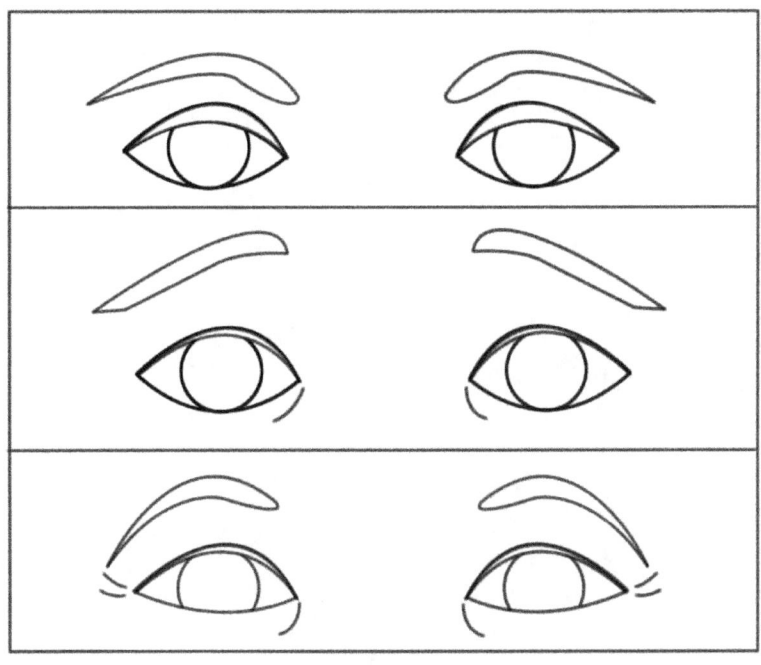

Noses

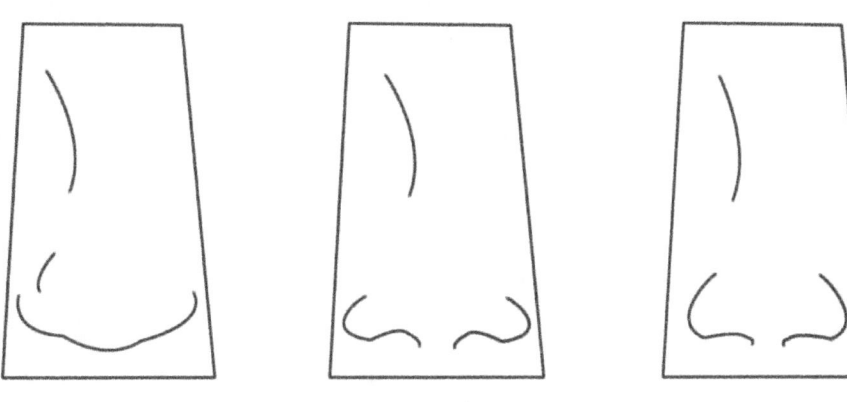

Mouths

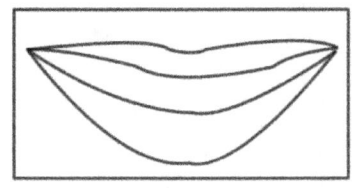 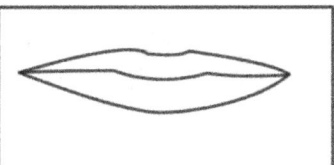 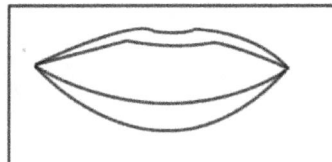

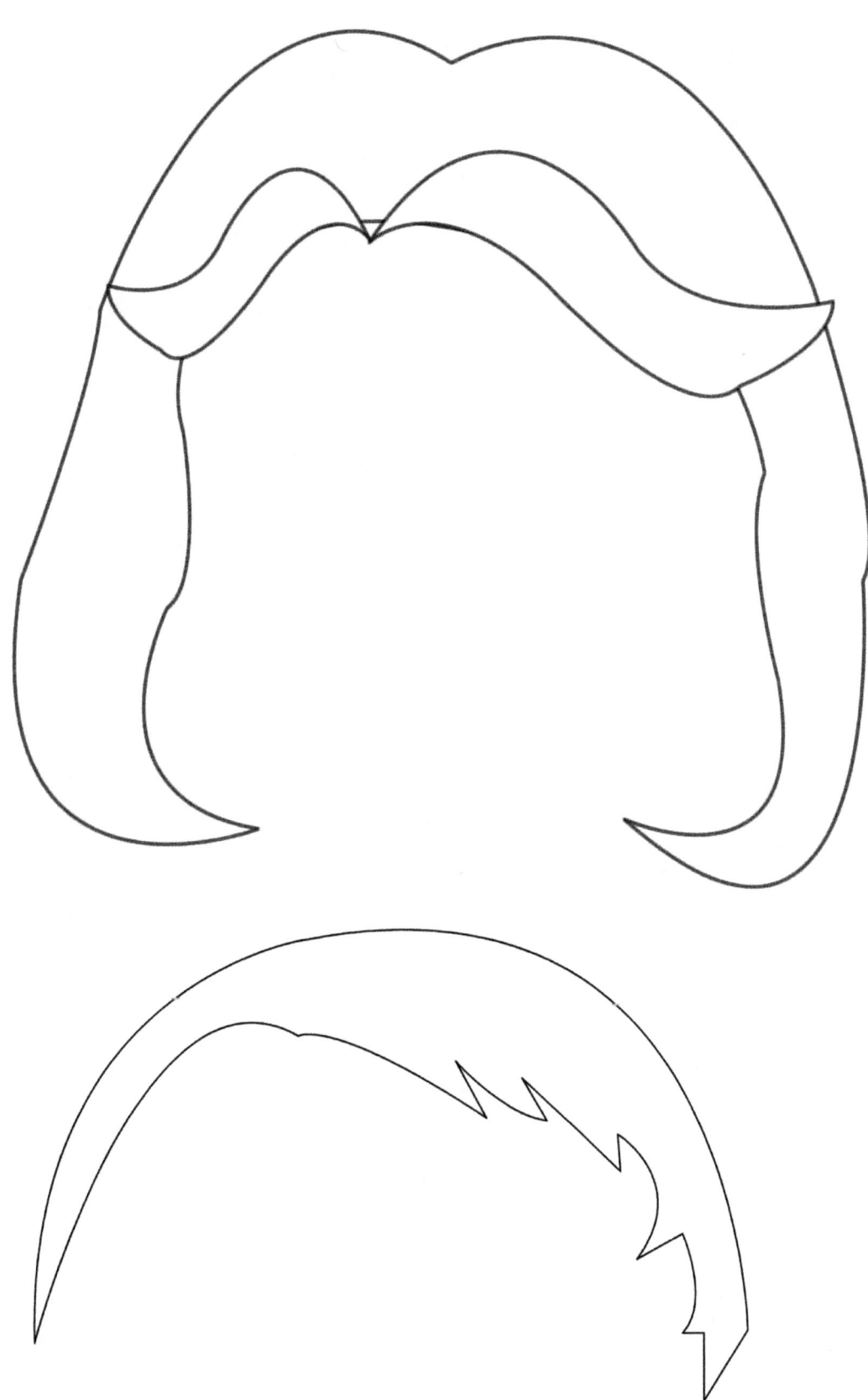

Lesson Eight

CREATING SECONDARY CHARACTERS WORKSHEET

Brave	Playful	Spunky	Jealous	Mysterious
Shy	Silly	Sneaky	Sad	Proud
Afraid	Sporty	Witty	Sneaky	Wise
Kind	Generous	Mean	Loud	Humble
Helpful	Sassy	Nice	Mischievous	Clumsy

Name several characters that you would like to add to the story:

a. **Name**: _____ Age: _____

Characteristics: You can choose from the list at the top of this worksheet or use your own words:
_____
_____

How do they know the main character? *Example: friend, parent, sibling, neighbor, cousin, teacher, stranger, etc.*

_____

b. **Name**: _____ Age: _____

Characteristics: You can choose from the list at the top of this worksheet or
use your own words:
_____
_____

How do they know the main character? *Example: friend, parent, sibling, neighbor, cousin, teacher, stranger, etc.*

_____

c. **Name**: _____ Age: _____

Characteristics: You can choose from the list at the top of this worksheet or use your own words:
_____
_____

How do they know the main character? Example: friend, parent, sibling, neighbor, cousin, teacher, stranger, etc.

_____

d. Name: _____ Age: _____

Characteristics: You can choose from the list at the top of this worksheet or use your own words:
_____
_____

How do they know the main character? Example: friend, parent, sibling, neighbor, cousin, teacher, stranger, etc.

_____

e. Name: _____ Age: _____

Characteristics: You can choose from the list at the top of this worksheet or use your own words:
_____
_____

How do they know the main character? Example: friend, parent, sibling, neighbor, cousin, teacher, stranger, etc.

_____

Lesson Nine

CREATING A PLOT WORKSHEET

> *"A good novel tells us the truth about its hero; but a bad novel tells us the truth about its author."*
> — G. K. Chesterton

1. Create a problem for your main character. Review your THEME *(Lesson Six)*:
___
___
___

2. Why does your character need to solve this?
___
___

3. What will be the first obstacle in his or her way?
___
___

4. How will he or she *almost* solve it?
___
___
___

5. How will that attempt fail?
___
___

6. How does your character feel now? Describe his or her actions that show this feeling.
___
___

7. How does your character finally reach his or her goal and overcome the problem?
___
___
___
___

Lesson Ten
CREATING DIALOGUE WORKSHEET

To get the most out of dialogue, you should use it to push the story along. Using empty dialogue is dry. You can use dialogue to tell something about your character.

"Penny, you never finish what you start." said mother.

"Do you really have to straighten the picture on the wall again? Can't you leave well enough alone?" said Father.

"Guard the castle while I am gone," said Tommy, as he pretended to swing a sword.

Practice using dialogue to tell about how your character looks:

Example: "I HATE my red hair!" pouted Carolyn as she stared in the mirror.

1. _____
2. _____
3. _____

Practice using dialogue to tell about what your character likes:

Example: "I can't wait to get my roller blades on and skate down to Jim's house," said Dan.

1. _____
2. _____

Practice using dialogue to tell what your character's personality is like:

- *For example: Happy, sad, greedy, giving, loving, or daring.*
- *Example: "No thanks, Mom," said Dan, "I don't feel like eating ice cream today."*

1. _____
2. _____
3. _____
4. _____
5. _____

Craft Time:

Let's create a short scene from your story in comic strip form. You can draw stick figures if you need to – the important thing is the dialogue! Use it to tell something about the character or describe a piece of action in the story.

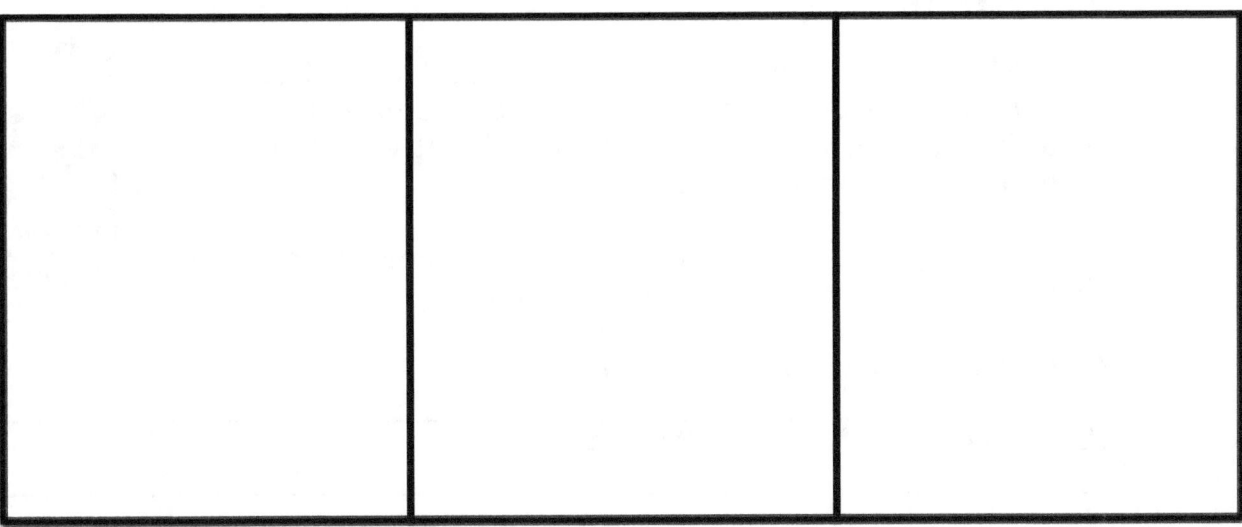

Create your comic strip in pencil, and then color it in with markers. Use black marker to the drawings and write the dialogue.

Sample Comic Strip:

Lesson Eleven

Great Beginnings!

Let's look at three different ways to start the story of *Little Red Riding Hood*:

> *"The life of every man is a diary in which he means to write one story, and writes another."*
> -James Matthew Barrie
> (author of Peter Pan)

Dialogue:

"Hurry, Red! Grandma's waiting to see you!" called Red Riding Hood's mother as she carefully packed a warm apple pie into a picnic basket. Mother had baked a pie from the harvest apples that Red had picked yesterday.

"Coming, Mother! Have you seen my red cape anywhere? It might be cooler in the forest where Grandma lives."

Which characters were introduced?

_____

List the words that describe the setting:

_____

Action:

"*SLAM* went the screen door as Little Red Riding Hood dashed out of her country cottage with a picnic basket on one arm and her cherry red cape tied around her neck. Her run slowed down to a skip when she remembered to be careful with the apple pie in her basket. She loved the way the red and gold leaves flew around her feet when she skipped."

Which characters were introduced?

_____

List the words that describe the setting:

_____

Description:

The sweet, spicy aroma of freshly baked apple pie reminded Red Riding Hood of the special day she planned with Grandma. She wondered if it would be cooler at Grandma's forest cottage than it was in her prairie home – maybe she should wear her favorite red cape! It would match the scarlet leaves on the maples trees that she would see on her way.

Which characters were introduced?

_____

List the words that describe the setting:

_____

Let's get started on our story…

Write your **OPENING SEGMENT** here. You can use a conversation between two characters, thoughts from the main character, a moment of action, or a descriptive passage to open your story. Be sure to include information about the setting. (See *Lesson Six.*)

_____
_____
_____
_____

Now add some **BACKGROUND INFORMATION** about the main character so that the reader can understand the rest of the story. (See *Lesson Seven.*)

_____
_____
_____
_____

Now tell about the **CONFLICT**. This is a good time to introduce **SECONDARY CHARACTERS**. (See *Lesson Nine* for the plot. Review *Lesson Ten* for using dialogue to tell the story and *Lesson Eight* for secondary characters.)

_____
_____
_____
_____
_____
_____
_____

Now tell about the **COMPLICATIONS**. (See *Lesson Nine and Ten.*)

_____
_____
_____
_____

_____
_____
_____
_____

Now tell about the **CLIMAX**. (See *Lessons Nine and Ten.*)

_____
_____
_____
_____
_____
_____
_____
_____

Now add the **CONCLUSION**. You might want to echo the **THEME** in this part:

_____
_____
_____
_____
_____
_____
_____

Hand in your workbooks to your teacher for editing when you are done. You will rewrite it during the next class.

Lesson Twelve

CREATING A TITLE WORKSHEET

Let's practice creating interesting titles by using the story of *Little Red Riding Hood*. Create a title for each aspect of the story. The first two have been done for you.

- The theme: *Dressing for Deception*

- The main character: *Little Red Riding Hood*

- The plot: _____

- The setting: _____

- A quote: _____

- A key object: _____

Now, write out six possible titles for your story, according to these six aspects:

- The theme:
  _____

- The main character:
  _____

- The plot: _____

- The setting: _____

- A quote: _____

- A key object: _____

Read them to your class or family and let them help you choose **the best one for your story**.

TITLE: _____

Craft Time:

You will now write your title and name on your cover page. Think about which type of writing will reflect your story's theme the best.

Cut out a title plate from white paper. Choose a shape that fits the feeling of the title (circle, oval, square, rectangle, or the shape of an object in your story, like a sailboat.)

Lightly write your title on the paper in pencil, and then go over it with markers, using Colors that go with your theme.

Be sure to add your name as the author!

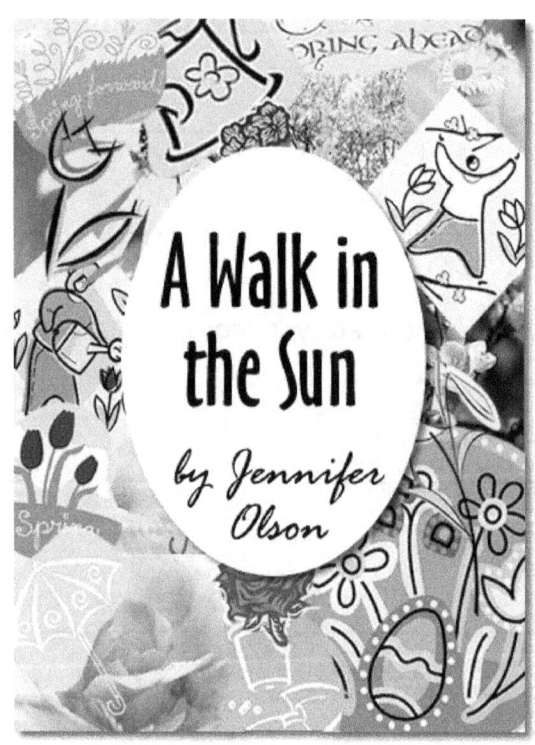

Look for More Fun New Millennium Kid's Writing Books- Turn Writing Time into a Delight!
www.NewMillenniumGirlBooks.com

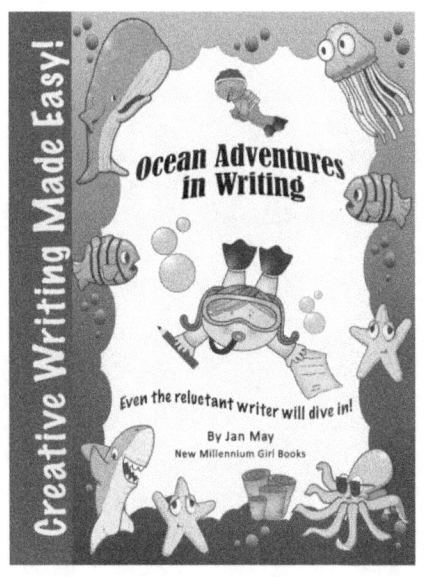

www.ingramcontent.com/pod-product-compliance
Lightning Source LLC
Chambersburg PA
CBHW060520300426
44112CB00017B/2738